from Frank Seward
All Hallows, 1963

WASHINGTON

CITY ON THE POTOMAC

Sketches by Fritz Busse

Text by Russell Baker

ARTS, INC., 667 MADISON AVENUE, NEW YORK 21, N.Y.

PUBLISHED IN THE UNITED STATES OF AMERICA

BY ARTS, INC.

LIBRARY OF CONGRESS CATALOG CARD NUMBER 58-11264

PRINTED IN GERMANY

First in war,
First in peace

Washington Monument
Flowing boulevards

and noble vistas
Pennsylvania Avenue

*When
in the Course of
human events ....*

IN CONGRESS, JULY 4, 1776.

The unanimous Declaration of the thirteen united States of America,

When in the Course of human events, it becomes necessary for one people to dissolve the political bands which have connected them with another, and to assume among the powers of the earth, the separate and equal station to which the Laws of Nature and of Nature's God entitle them, a decent respect to the opinions of mankind requires that they should declare the causes which impel them to the separation. — We hold these truths to be self-evident, that all men are created equal, that they are endowed by their Creator with certain unalienable Rights, that among these are Life, Liberty and the pursuit of Happiness. — That to secure these rights, Governments are instituted among Men, deriving their just powers from the consent of the governed, — That whenever any Form of Government becomes destructive of these ends, it is the Right of the People to alter or to abolish it, and to institute new Government, laying its foundation on such principles and organizing its powers in such form, as to them shall seem most likely to effect their Safety and Happiness. Prudence, indeed, will dictate that Governments long established should not be changed for light and transient causes; and accordingly all experience hath shewn, that mankind are more disposed to suffer, while evils are sufferable, than to right themselves by abolishing the forms to which they are accustomed. But when a long train of abuses and usurpations, pursuing invariably the same Object evinces a design to reduce them under absolute Despotism, it is their right, it is their duty, to throw off such Government, and to provide new Guards for their future security. — Such has been the patient sufferance of these Colonies; and such is now the necessity which constrains them to alter their former Systems of Government. The history of the present King of Great Britain is a history of repeated injuries and usurpations, all having in direct object the establishment of an absolute Tyranny over these States. To prove this, let Facts be submitted to a candid world. — He has refused his Assent to Laws, the most wholesome and necessary for the public good. — He has forbidden his Governors to pass Laws of immediate and pressing importance, unless suspended in their operation till his Assent should be obtained; and when so suspended, he has utterly neglected to attend to them. — He has refused to pass other Laws for the accommodation of large districts of people, unless those people would relinquish the right of Representation in the Legislature, a right inestimable to them and formidable to tyrants only. — He has called together legislative bodies at places unusual, uncomfortable, and distant from the depository of their public Records, for the sole purpose of fatiguing them into compliance with his measures. — He has dissolved Representative Houses repeatedly, for opposing with manly firmness his invasions on the rights of the people. — He has refused for a long time, after such dissolutions, to cause others to be elected; whereby the Legislative powers, incapable of Annihilation, have returned to the People at large for their exercise; the State remaining in the mean time exposed to all the dangers of invasion from without, and convulsions within. — He has endeavoured to prevent the population of these States; for that purpose obstructing the Laws for Naturalization of Foreigners; refusing to pass others to encourage their migrations hither, and raising the conditions of new Appropriations of Lands. — He has obstructed the Administration of Justice, by refusing his Assent to Laws for establishing Judiciary powers. — He has made Judges dependent on his Will alone, for the tenure of their offices, and the amount and payment of their salaries. — He has erected a multitude of New Offices, and sent hither swarms of Officers to harrass our people, and eat out their substance. — He has kept among us, in times of peace, Standing Armies without the Consent of our legislatures. — He has affected to render the Military independent of and superior to the Civil power. — He has combined with others to subject us to a jurisdiction foreign to our constitution, and unacknowledged by our laws; giving his Assent to their Acts of pretended Legislation: — For Quartering large bodies of armed troops among us: — For protecting them, by a mock Trial, from punishment for any Murders which they should commit on the Inhabitants of these States: — For cutting off our Trade with all parts of the world: — For imposing Taxes on us without our Consent: — For depriving us in many cases, of the benefits of Trial by Jury: — For transporting us beyond Seas to be tried for pretended offences — For abolishing the free System of English Laws in a neighbouring Province, establishing therein an Arbitrary government, and enlarging its Boundaries so as to render it at once an example and fit instrument for introducing the same absolute rule into these Colonies: — For taking away our Charters, abolishing our most valuable Laws, and altering fundamentally the Forms of our Governments: — For suspending our own Legislatures, and declaring themselves invested with power to legislate for us in all cases whatsoever. — He has abdicated Government here, by declaring us out of his Protection and waging War against us. — He has plundered our seas, ravaged our Coasts, burnt our towns, and destroyed the lives of our people. — He is at this time transporting large Armies of foreign Mercenaries to compleat the works of death, desolation and tyranny, already begun with circumstances of Cruelty & perfidy scarcely paralleled in the most barbarous ages, and totally unworthy the Head of a civilized nation. — He has constrained our fellow Citizens taken Captive on the high Seas to bear Arms against their Country, to become the executioners of their friends and Brethren, or to fall themselves by their Hands. — He has excited domestic insurrections amongst us, and has endeavoured to bring on the inhabitants of our frontiers, the merciless Indian Savages, whose known rule of warfare, is an undistinguished destruction of all ages, sexes and conditions. In every stage of these Oppressions We have Petitioned for Redress in the most humble terms: Our repeated Petitions have been answered only by repeated injury. A Prince, whose character is thus marked by every act which may define a Tyrant, is unfit to be the ruler of a free people. Nor have We been wanting in attentions to our Brittish brethren. We have warned them from time to time of attempts by their legislature to extend an unwarrantable jurisdiction over us. We have reminded them of the circumstances of our emigration and settlement here. We have appealed to their native justice and magnanimity, and we have conjured them by the ties of our common kindred to disavow these usurpations, which, would inevitably interrupt our connections and correspondence. They too have been deaf to the voice of justice and of consanguinity. We must, therefore, acquiesce in the necessity, which denounces our Separation, and hold them, as we hold the rest of mankind, Enemies in War, in Peace Friends. —

We, therefore, the Representatives of the united States of America, in General Congress, Assembled, appealing to the Supreme Judge of the world for the rectitude of our intentions, do, in the Name, and by Authority of the good People of these Colonies, solemnly publish and declare, That these United Colonies are, and of Right ought to be Free and Independent States; that they are Absolved from all Allegiance to the British Crown, and that all political connection between them and the State of Great Britain, is and ought to be totally dissolved; and that as Free and Independent States, they have full Power to levy War, conclude Peace, contract Alliances, establish Commerce, and to do all other Acts and Things which Independent States may of right do. — And for the support of this Declaration, with a firm reliance on the protection of divine Providence, we mutually pledge to each other our Lives, our Fortunes and our sacred Honor.

John Hancock

Button Gwinnett
Lyman Hall
Geo Walton.

Wm Hooper
Joseph Hewes,
John Penn

Edward Rutledge.
Thos Heyward Junr.
Thomas Lynch Junr.
Arthur Middleton

Samuel Chase
Wm. Paca
Thos. Stone
Charles Carroll of Carrollton

George Wythe
Richard Henry Lee
Th Jefferson
Benja. Harrison
Thos Nelson jr.
Francis Lightfoot Lee
Carter Braxton

Robt Morris
Benjamin Rush
Benja. Franklin
John Morton
Geo Clymer
Jas. Smith.
Geo. Taylor
James Wilson
Geo. Ross
Caesar Rodney
Geo Read
Tho M:Kean

Wm Floyd
Phil. Livingston
Frans. Lewis
Lewis Morris
Richd. Stockton
Jno Witherspoon
Fras. Hopkinson
John Hart
Abra Clark

Josiah Bartlett
Wm. Whipple
Saml Adams
John Adams
Robt Treat Paine
Elbridge Gerry
Step. Hopkins
William Ellery
Roger Sherman
Sam.el Huntington
Wm. Williams
Oliver Wolcott
Matthew Thornton

Library of Congress

Capitol Hill

Green Island of Loneliness

FROM BABYLON TO THE NEW WORLD

From Babylon to London, history's fabled capitals have distilled their nations' memories and dreams and from the essence taken character unique to themselves. With Washington it is not yet so.

Paris, London, Berlin—these are cities superficially alien to the lands beyond their very gates, yet so palpably products of their nations' spirits that they forever typify England, Germany, France before the world.

Here in the New World, on the big gliding bend of the Potomac, out of wilderness and bog where no natural city could otherwise have risen, men have created a capital with little independent spirit of her own, but with wonderful capacity to mirror, chameleon-like, the ever-shifting mood and spirit of America.

But for the rare and little-heeded native, the Washingtonian is foremost a citizen of the continent. His nerve-ends reach into villages, Main Streets, ghettos and cross-roads from Nag's Head to Cucamonga. Quick to sense, Washington is quick to respond to the national urge of the moment.

When America is smug, Washington is smugger; when America sickens with fear, Washington finds victims for immolation in her terrible arenas; when America angers, Washington goes to her great reservoirs of energy, imagination, daring, to do fantastic deeds. When America gropes for idealism, Washington steadies foundering nations, offers haven and hope for the hopeless, attracts a Lincoln to add ennobling human dimensions to democracy.

But for the truly perceptive, the visitor will fail to sense the continental forces commanding the tide of the city's life. To read a nation's pulse is a thing that takes time and great experience and, so, Washington is not to be felt immediately as the traveler, on first contact, feels New York's vitality, Chicago's brute strength, San Francisco's gossamer charm.

The tourist pilgrim will take away an image of green-cloaked marbled shrines, of vast thoroughfares reminiscent of Paris but for the overhanging elm and oak and, perhaps, of cool silences in rooms where the breath of history floats like dust in a sunbeam.

"A gracious, pleasing city to the eye", the cosmopolite will say, having seen the drama of the Capitol's pearl-gray dome floodlit against a moonless winter night, or the airy minaret of the Moslem mosque against a backdrop of gleaming apartment buildings at twilight. "But so provincial! No theater! No place for the artist! No night life!"

And he, too, will be right, for Washington's business is government and politics, and all else is subsidiary. To the other endeavors that humanize men it is not inhospitable, but indifferent. Its own business is vital, all-absorbing, and it has patience for little else. The artist seeking creative and intellectual air will look elsewhere. The chief qualifications for Washington's business are judgment, occasional rapacity, zest for hard work, but rarely intellectuality, cultivation or creativity.

In form and in spirit, Washington is an arena. Lying in a huge natural amphitheatre formed by hills beyond and river before, she is built for combat. Here men contend in that most competitive of all human activities, the struggle for power. For many of her people, combat for survival is the routine of daily life.

Many, inevitably, are debased by the contest or flounder on personal incompetence or stupidity; these give the city its flamboyant reputation for wanton viciousness and asininity. Most, unnoticed, accommodate the demands of survival with codes of decency; these give the city its middle-class solidity.

A few raise ideals above survival, to be widely despised in their own time and enshrined by generations afterwards.

The aesthetic will carp at the pretentious, Graeco-Roman bulk of her architecture and ask why she chose an Egyptian obelisk to memorialize George Washington, Greek columns for the backwoodsman Lincoln, Roman dome for the revolutionist Jefferson.

Acting for a young people, self-conscious at the wonder of their succeeding experiment, she has built in a way alien to her pioneer tradition, but guaranteed to endure.

Thus, when the White House was found collapsing, it was not razed and reconstructed as the modern office structure with penthouse apartment that Presidents now require. Instead it was restored as the remembered calm and lovely Colonial home, antique and lonely in a quiet island of green, where a man could meet Destiny in the privacy of his living-room.

Yet, but for the formal shrines, there are few places left to remind the hurried that history has walked these lawns and boulevards. So absorbed in the present that she scarcely has time to consider the future, Washington has let much of her visible past go down. Like the nation, she is still too young to treasure and cherish her memories; the square that older capitals would preserve is allowed to die here, victim to the modern fever for fresh buildings, functional lines and glass expanses.

For behind the facade of sleepy Southern streets and relaxed urbanity, this, even more than New York, is a city of furies. On Capitol Hill men strive to soothe corrosive passions that drive a headstrong people.

In the Supreme Court nine men labor not only to preserve the ancient legacy, but to find its truth for today. Washington's arms circle the globe, too, and men lie awake haunted by what could happen in Damascus or Saigon, by production slowdowns on the newest engine of death, by today's Stock Market report or a rise in the British bank rate, by unemployment in Detroit, an assassination in the Caribbean, starvation in Calcutta.

Someday perhaps it will be pleasant to look back and remember this time. But memories are for the old and Washington, still a mere 160, is impatient to move on. She has little time now to look back and dream.

Symbol of a Nation's Aspirations

Gothic quiet
in a city of furies
Washington Cathedral

Lincoln - Memorial

Cherry blossom time

Classic reflections - Lincoln Memorial

Here and there, a glimpse of Parisian grace

R.S.V.P. and intrigue – Embassy row

Connecticut avenue shoppers

Even as American cities count time, Washington is young. She dates her age from mid-June, 1800, when "the seat of government" moved in from Philadelphia. The Government, now so vast that it has long since overflowed the city's "ten square miles" and washed into Virginia and Maryland, was then a bureaucracy of 126 men.

The site of its new home, much of it a fen at the Potomac's confluence with the Anacostia River, had been, like much of the history since written here, a compromise choice to soothe an angry South.

At her very birth, L'Enfant, the French visionary, had outraged the landholders and astounded the Founding Fathers with a city plan as grandiose as Wren's for rebuilding burned London. L'Enfant's plan is still the basic drawing of today's Twentieth Century capital, but the men of 1800, seeing only wilderness and farmland where the Frenchman had envisioned grand avenues and magnificent buildings, eventually dismissed him as an impractical dreamer.

A collection of "small miserable huts", wrote one dismayed Cabinet member fresh from sophisticated Philadelphia. "You may look in almost any direction, over an extent of ground nearly as large as the city of New York, without seeing a fence or any object except brick-kilns and temporary huts for laborers."

For nearly half a century, Washington remained a Southern village centered around Lafayette Square before the White House and sprawling out to the unfinished Capitol on the East and old Georgetown to the West.

These boundaries are less than the inner nucleus of today's city. What was an afternoon ride in the country for Lincoln is now a quick taxi trip to Walter Reed Hospital. Georgetown, a bustling Potomac port when Americans still looked to London for government, is now a sheltered downtown residential quarter.

South across the Potomac, land once occupied by Confederate troops now lies minutes from the White House along looping ribbons of concrete. To the north and west, the city has thrust L'Enfant's great boulevards into lands that were rustic countryside less than a century ago and adorned them with great apartment blocks and palatial embassies.

From the northeast the city pokes groping fingers towards Baltimore, forty miles away. Already more than half of her two million live without the boundary lines drawn by her founders. And still she grows.

The visitor must bring an acute sense of history if

he would catch the smell of the past under this sleek and glistening patina of modernity. Standing in Lafayette Square on an April night, it is still possible to envision the murderous Paine of the Lincoln assassination gang flee, panting and bloody from his frenzy, out of Secretary Seward's old home and dash eastward towards escape.

It is not so easy, standing in the present-day bustle of Pennsylvania Avenue just below the old Ford's Theater, to feel the chill rush of John Wilkes Booth's ghost galloping that same April night south towards the river.

Or, to stand today beyond the impersonal barred lawn of the White House, so distant and aloof, and catch the faroff echo of backwoods laughter and breaking crockery that Inauguration night when Andy Jackson let America into the "presidential palace".

At the Capitol, you can still feel how it must have been with Webster and Hayne tuning the language to an ominous rumble and the bitter, brilliant, slowly-dying Calhoun looking on. Walk into any Senate hearing room and close your eyes and listen and you can almost see the midget perched on the startled J. P. Morgan's lap.

But most of the truly great moments can be recaptured only by complete exercise of the imagination, for history has begun to move here like a whirlwind and a century back seems more like a thousand light years ago, the 1920 s' like an old dimly remembered dream.

Calvin Coolidge in his rocking chair? No. Impossible that the President could ever have been able just to sit and rock. Mr. Jefferson riding horseback up Capitol Hill for his Inaugural? British troops firing the White House? Abigail Adams hanging her wash to dry in the cavernous White House state rooms?

These must be taken on faith and record, for they belong to the city of another era that now seems more remote than the Tiberian orgies seem to the modern traveler standing in Rome's ruined Colosseum.

The reality in this new city is the 300-horsepower limousine and the unlimited expense account, the transcontinental airliner over the Capitol, the secret agent and the forty billion dollar military budget, the ghost writer and the split atom.

Rocking chairs, horses and clotheslines have become curios in this new city, to be sought by the musty-minded in museums. What remains of the past are tradition and ideal.

The memories, except in the archives and the books, have been too fragile to endure.

Night drama

Federal Triangle . . . Bureaucracy's Citadel

Where nine defend an ancient legacy – Supreme Court

Muffled drums and awesome stillness
Arlington National Cemetery

Eighteenth century cameo - Mount Vernon

Lafayette Square before the White House

Revolutionary's shrine - Jefferson Memorial

Indian God at National Gallery evokes a primitive tradition

NORTH, EAST, SOUTH, WEST

Though geographically bound to the industrial Northeast, Washington is still unmistakably a creature of the American South. The native accent is Southern; the pace of her pedestrians, leisurely.

In spring she is a blaze of brilliant, bursting azalea and rhododendron and glittering yellow forsythia, and in the gracious homes of the Northwest on a close summer evening when the locusts sing the promise of tomorrow's heat, men sit to dine by candlelight under the trees.

Nearly half the inner city's people now are Negro; they endow her posture with their race's indolent grace, her voice with the rich drawl of the South, her temperament with their infinite humor and sanity.

In mid-summer the winds blow off the Carolinas and stifle the city under layers of breathless damp heat; the sound of the city becomes the throb of the air-conditioner multiplied ten-thousandfold like the purring of some disembodied monster.

Like any Confederate town, her floral centerpiece, Lafayette Square, is a tree-shaded splash of green for pigeons and idlers, dominated by a revered military hero—not a Confederate general, to be sure, but General Andrew Jackson heroically sitting his metal charger.

Like a lady of the ante-bellum South, the city has learned to present herself with graciousness, dignity and gentility. Her chief ornaments are her trees. She has used them to soften her contours and cool her acres of concrete and asphalt, to shade her homes and change her colors with the seasons and to express her moods under the passing of the elements.

Thus when a hurricane lurched in from the sea some years ago, the city became the field of a spectacular, shrieking battle between the wind and the trees, a raging green ocean of howling treetops. A few were sucked from the ground and hurled away like discarded matchsticks. But these were few and by night, as durable as the city, the trees stood serene as the brilliant-starred sky that followed the storm.

Somewhere in these pages the artist has caught the peculiarly Southern indolence of the city as she begins her annual rebirth, with the blooming of the fragile pink white of the cherry blossoms over the Tidal Basin. With another, of kittens waiting among scattered leaves on a Georgetown patio, he has captured the mood of her decline into winter when the wind shifts to the north, returns the scattered politicians and brings the city her season of Northern business and bustle.

Yet even in these times the South is never far removed. for the patriarchs who give character to the Congress, and so to much of the city, are mostly the men of the South. Their control of Capitol Hill is proprietary. The way of life they bring to the city is little affected by the upstarts from North and West whose stay, due to the dangers of two-party politics, is seldom long.

In this city where the war was led that crushed the South, it is not unsettling that the home of Robert E. Lee should be the dominating landmark of the near Virginia hillside, looking down on the very spot where Americans have built their shrine to Lincoln.

Take the steamer from the riverfront down to Mount Vernon and you stand before Washington's pre-Revolutionary mansion, still little-changed since the era of the slave-owning Virginia aristocracy.

Or, on a spring day when the oaks are full, you can still be towed languidly behind slow-plodding mules along the old C & O Canal paralleling the Potomac through the city into Georgetown.

Georgetown itself, and Alexandria across the Potomac, are residential shades of the colonial South, with their narrow, cool, shaded streets and lovingly restored Eighteenth Century simplicity. Washingtonians who prefer living among reminders of days when life was less shrill compete for space in these sheltered retreats. And on Capitol Hill, real-estate men are re-creating more.

It is the American Midwest rather than the cosmopolitan Northeast that has had the greatest secondary impact on the city's life. This, too, is not surprising, for the true capital of the East has always been Philadelphia or New York while the Midwest, with its parental claim to the Republican Party, has divided its attention between Chicago and the Potomac.

Downtown Washington, with its flat, square, graceless skyline and genial provincialism, is but one remove from any Main Street in Iowa. The big rambling frame homes of Chevy Chase and the less pretentious brick homes of Northwest Washington's elmed and mapled sidestreets are more akin to a small Indiana town than to Manhattan.

On a summer Sunday morning here, you can hear the bang of a screendoor, the cries of small boys playing baseball in the big backyards, the echo of a family's footsteps down a shady sidewalk on the way to worship.

This external city, a blend of South and Midwest, seems deceptively remote from the furied stir that is its people's business.

Georgetown University

Hushed secluded streets for solitary reflection

Indian summer bus stop

In
Georgetown shops
even dolls must charm

Colonial survivor

STAR GRILL
MIXED GRILL
NO PAR KING
MAME SEA FOOD
SUBMARINE 50¢
MAINE CARRY OUT SEA FOOD
ENTRANCE CARRY OUT
LOBSTER
SHRIMP HOUSE
WATER FRONT
CARRY OUT
B.

Riverfront

Alexandria pastoral

C & O Canal mirrors the city of the past

For all her external placidity, the Washington of this generation, freshly embarked on a global career more astounding than the Founding Fathers ever conceived, may have entered her Golden Age.

Unprepared, almost unawares, she has become the focus of the world's fear and hope, a global crossroads where monarchs pause and the polyglot peoples of the earth gather to assist the shaping of their destinies.

It is a new role and the city is still unfamiliar in it and a bit self-conscious to find herself, unrehearsed, at center stage. Her attempts at pomp still teeter on the edge of comic disaster, saved only by her underlying genius for goodhumored republican informality.

Looking back some day, historians may write of it as one of mankind's fantastic cities, an exotic blend of cosmopolis and small town where men could debate with equal fury a policy towards India or the efficacy of a battery additive.

And what exotic sights she affords! Prime Ministers and Presidents troop to the White House so frequently that they scarcely attract press notices. The Queen of England, unapproachable in her own domain, pauses here to clasp hands with the impecunious hundreds of the press.

Some time back, casual pedestrians, glancing up, could see the King of Arabia, clad in flowing black-and-white goldtrimmed desert robes, strolling through light winter snow, trailed by scowling desert warriors with jewel-sheathed daggers against their chests.

In the State Department's bureaucratic corridors you may encounter a group of touring Asian journalists, speaking for papers from Tokyo to Karachi. Or, in its press room, find a man from Moscow kibitzing a poker hand among a Frenchman, a Swiss, a Polish refugee, a Chinese, and a second-generation Italian.

In the solemn rococo corridors of the Capitol at springtime, the frozen statues of dead statesmen look down on swarms of high-school students from Butte and Keokuk and Macon.

Boys in T-shirts, girls often in electric-bright drum-majorette tights – the costume of the high-school pilgrims – the youth from the hinterland inspecting their government remind the forgetful of the raucous fresh strength that drives the country.

The city has become a magnet to the world, which washes against it in waves of humanity across Union Station's vast vaulted waiting rooms or descends from the skies as the airliners rumble around the clock into National Airport.

The flow is ceaseless now.

All who have a cause eventually find Washington the place to press it; thus the city is filled with human clamor. The lobbyist, he who lives by his wits, the animal lover, the movie queen a-prowl for publicity, men who want to halt the consumption of alcohol and men who want to increase it, idealists, hate-peddlers, free-traders and protectionists—all contribute voices to the din.

And the din, too, is ceaseless.

Men who command industrial empires perfume the White House lobby with cigar smoke. Thugs, scoundrels and innocent sacrificial victims come to the Capitol to undergo the ordeal of the television lights and the headline hunter.

In the crystalled salons of the Northwest, moneyed ladies seeking status-by-association compete for Supreme Court Justices, Senators, Ambassadors and Cabinet officers in the ritualistic dogfight of official social life. Somewhere, too, understood but by a few, espionage and counter-espionage are played out in the shadows.

The big Embassy staffs have internationalized many areas of this onetime Capital of Isolationism. Almost invariably, however, Washington affects them more strongly than they affect Washington.

Thus it is common to see a small boy from Thailand or Yugoslavia or Brazil, in cowboy hat or black-leather jacket, fluent in the newest American slang, diving for a football or heading off small American hombres at Eagle Pass. In their homelands, their parents may have despised the materialism of American life; in Washington, they are quick to acquire chrome-plastered cars with jukebox styling and homes as automatic as American materialism can afford.

Some drawn here are touching. Such is the defeated veteran of the Washington political wars. During his active career in politics, you may be sure, he was quick to rail at the city's wastrel ways before the home folk and to compare it odiously with the sweet charm of his native vote-giving soil.

Once out of office, his melody changes. The fallen son of this or those hills becomes suddenly, shockingly, aware that his personal roots are no longer out there among the votes, that they have put down here and that he is, of all things, a Washingtonian.

Most settle and stay on, working out careers at law or lobbying. On opening days of Congress you see them banded in wistful tableaux, standing to the rear of the Senate chamber, watching the new that has made them old.

"They never go back to Pocatello", it is said of those that Government has hurled aside. And it is true. They rarely do. For all its clamor, perhaps because of it, Washington affects people that way.

Easy afternoon

Lee Mansion — Kitchen

Lee Mansion well house

Minutes from the atom era a breath of the ante-bellum South

Colonial Georgetown in Autumn gown

Christ Church; Alexandria

In the Franciscan monastery garden

Chesapeake and Ohio Canal still forms a ghostly water boulevard to the old city

From gentle Virginia hills
the city seems a shimmering mirage

CITY OF MANY FACES

The city has many faces, many sounds; some of repelling squalor, some of great beauty, some visible and audible only to the inner senses. These last go unseen, unheard by most who come to the city today, for they are too busy to look or to listen for them. It is easy to walk the blighted inner city's teeming streets, awash with the stench of poverty, and see the squalid profile the guide books never mention.

So, too, for her beauties. From the air at night she drifts under the plane's wing like a vast web of softly jeweled lights spun in the darkness below. From atop Washington's monument, she is sun-washed vistas of bone-white and forest-green and noble boulevards criss-crossing between river and hill.

From up there the eye is led downward into the impregnable three-sided fortress of bureaucracy that is Federal Triangle, the bastion built to "red tape". Or, another direction, down into the glens of northern Virginia and along the serene, little-traveled Potomac.

In Rock Creek Park, cutting across the city's northwest quadrant, she has preserved a remnant of her wilderness face. There the searcher for solitude can still find primeval silences minutes from the traffic's yawp; among towering oaks, hear the variations in a bird's chatter, study the sound the creek makes against its shadowed, pebbled bed.

In the downtown's evening rush, the newcomer may conclude from the hurry of office-workers and the traffic's snarling confusion that this is a city of huge vitality, not unlike New York.

A few hours later, when the city has withdrawn behind her residential doors to indulge her peculiarly private social ways, he may find the same streets abandoned and wonder at the provincialism that lets the city die at evening. If Manhattan's night sound is the cry of the trumpet against canyon walls, downtown Washington's is the echo of dispirited footfalls off half-deserted streets.

And there are the sounds, the scenes that only the few will catch.

The echo of the depression Army tramping to do battle with the 1930s' bonus marchers; the all-but-forgotten curses of hungry, desperate men blinded by tear-gas, routed from the capital as enemies of the Republic.

The awful tension that tautened the city's nerves in July, 1863, as she waited for news of the outcome at Gettysburg to know her fate. The sound of the cheering in the old Willard Hotel dining room two years later as

Grant, fresh from Appomattox and still flustered by fame, entered for dinner. And half a century later, the cool, brutal surgery performed by Senator Lodge at Capitol Hill to dismantle Wilson's dream.

The city has other faces, other sounds, that are more distinct. The deadened thud of black, muffled drums, the creak of the horse-drawn caisson in National Cemetery as the nation buries its fighting men; the lonely despair of the bugler's "Taps" piercing the cool, green stillness.

And on Inauguration Days on the Capitol steps, the one man who can speak for the people repeating the old oath: "I--- do solemnly swear---".

And before the yellowed old document, the voices of schoolboys puzzling out the ancient words, still thunderous on the ear: "When in the course of human events ---".

As a city, Washington may still not have found and distilled the essence of America as other, older capitals have defined the spirits of their nations. She may be still no more than the sum of a nation's parts, secondary in the affections of her people.

Yet, she is faithful and quick to reflect the momentary aspirations of her nation, and capable always of reminding it of the nobler, older ones and of the price of their fulfillment.

To see her best is to see her detached from the frenzy of humanity that is her business, to see her as the enduring symbol of the nation's past and future. The best place is from the crest of the first Virginia hills beyond the river. From there, she lies low in the river valley, silent and seemingly empty.

Her skyline is dominated by two widely-spaced hills which men have capped with facing monuments to their faith and hope.

One hill raises the Capitol's mighty dome against the sky; the other, the old Gothic lines of the Washington Cathedral. Between them when the sun is bright and the air rises in wavering streaks of heat, the city seems a shimmering, sunken island of green where men have erected domes and columns and spires, and then vanished and left them dreaming in the sun, as antique as the human yearning for freedom.

From the Virginia silences, it is hushed, motionless and, through the heat haze, as unreal as the Baghdad of the fables.

What fantasies, you wonder, might not befall in such a place?

Colonial Georgetown in green spring gown

World Capital – rear door

Citizen of Leisure

Waiting for the teatime guests to leave

Politics! Politics! Politics!

The Potomac's Gliding Entry to the City

Riverside retreat in Potomac quiet

Great falls of the
Potomac
beyond the city